all i did was listen

rachel awes

rachel awes ✤

isbn 978-1-1-4675-4772-7

all i did was listen
p.o. box 4422
saint paul, mn 55104
usa

www.allididwaslisten.com
www.rachelawes.etsy.com
rachelawes@gmail.com

printed in the united states of america by signature book printing.
www.sbpbooks.com

a space of listening.

"no one listens, they tell me,
'so i listen...
'i tell them
what they have just told me,
'i sit in silence,
listening to them,
letting them grieve.
'julian, you are wise,'
they say, ~
'you have been gifted
with understanding.'
all i did was listen.
for i believe full surely
that God's spirit
is in us all..."
julian of norwich

✳ introduction ✳
(in six parts)

✳ people come into therapy, both young + old, with burdens on their beautiful hearts. they speak of pressures at work, stress in relationships, losing a loved one, feeling disconnected from God, feeling they are wasting breathing time on this planet, + so on. whether presented initially or not, the most common + deepest thread of pain i hear is loneliness.

(one)

❀ there are many ways
loneliness is expressed.
one person typed out
an organized list of
concerns, complete with
bullet points, +then set
apart from the rest of
her list read:
  " i   a m   a l o n e."
another person longs to
have a best friend, +
another a lover. others
have plenty of people
nearby but no one is
really listening to them
either.
          (two)
          ❀

✳ all i do is pull up a chair, lean in, + listen. i am on the look out for the gold that has been long forgotten because no one has been around to remind them of it. i ask them:

"did you hear what you just said ?! "

+

"do you hear how wise + beautiful you are ?! "

(three)

✳

* gold is just what i have
found. just like when i was
young + gathered up swirly
caramel-looking agates +
marbles holding magical rainbows inside, i have now
gathered up these.
* (g)listening stories.
i have distilled quotes/
paraphrases/captions from a
number of clients in this
book but not from all of
them, + yet i intend for
the spirit of every one to be
honored in these pages.
(four)

✽ i thank them for their consent. i thank them for inspiring me to wake up + be more present in my own life + appreciate the great gifts of love where i find them, to be more honest when lost, to be braver with feeling my feelings, to say what is really on my mind, + to hold greater intention + attention.

(five)

✽

✳ i now offer them to
you, the reader. my hope
is to pass on such
affirmation of the great
life that is within us
all. this is an invitation
to listen. the beauty
within is truly
        astounding~
    even, +maybe especially,
out of the hidden +
painful places.
        (six)
        ✳

seven chapters ✳

four. room for flowers

five. hold hands

six. a clear stream running

seven. i am who i am who i am

secret key

living out of beauty

i want to take the same care with myself that beatrix potter did in drawing peter rabbit. i want to use soft lines. loving words. kind eyes. give myself sweet pals. merry adventures. fresh carrots.

i will begin by placing colored pencils in my purse to remind me.

☆ treasured = client quote

" i have realized that i haven't been taking care of myself because i have been living out of my blah instead of my beauty."

☆ my reflection for you

✳ my art playground ding for ♡ you

to live out of

i am resolved

my beauty.

one

messiness inside *

messiness inside

we glimpse our messiness as we wake up.
tangled + tousled hair. sleepy lines on skin.
wrinkled pajamas. uneven
steps. here we all are in our
glorious realness.

this is the us fresh from
dreams. the place where we
don't censor. the place where
we are wolves + bears + fly in
fields + swim with whales +
chase down intruders + travel
to the place of everywhere
to be just who we are. in
dreams we see our whole life
tumble out in front of us + our
beauty is in the entirety of
our story + we don't need to
fix anything. transformation comes in the truth
telling. in being seen + accepted where we are
right now.

o that i could tell myself, day + night, my whole
story with no shame. chase down my truest tell
+ embrace my allness.

"i like not having order everywhere + i want to embrace having some messiness inside."

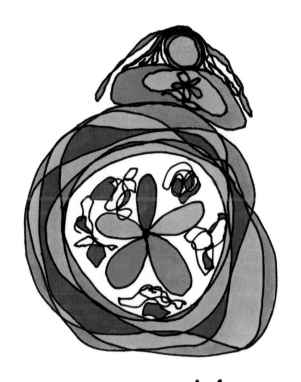

we all
start here....
honest. bare.
    & immensely interesting.

dumping all i got

women carry a bunch of truth telling in their purses. imagine
we all sit in a circle + dump out our contents. here are a few
of mine...

loose smooshed milk duds. mint gum + random wrappers.
lip-gloss. a note that says, "you are loved". driving directions.

what might this begin to
reveal? maybe that i enjoy
sweets + also lose track of
all i treasure. it even gets
smooshed sometimes. i value
shining + love being loved + i
can get anxious about getting
places. what is in yours?

let's put all our contents into
the light + send ourselves +
each other simple hums of
yes + i see you.

even the sunflowers know
about putting it all in the light.
maybe they are too chattering about what's in their purses.
together buzzing like a field of cicadas.

(a lot of love love love love).

...sending love to all that comes tumbling out

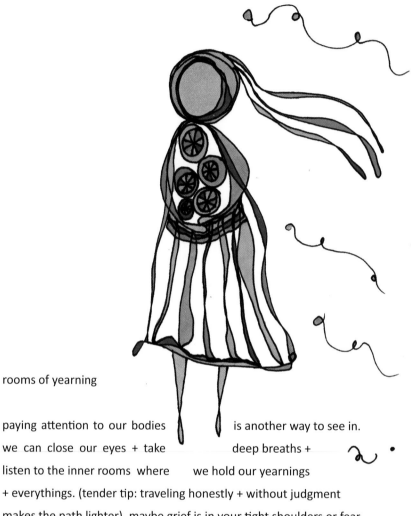

rooms of yearning

paying attention to our bodies   is another way to see in.
we can close our eyes + take   deep breaths +
listen to the inner rooms where   we hold our yearnings
+ everythings. (tender tip: traveling honestly + without judgment
makes the path lighter). maybe grief is in your tight shoulders or fear
in your unsettled stomach. your body tells your story.

go in + open windows. let the wind witness + refresh you. decorate if
you wish. anything is possible. even moroccan lanterns.

"there is a room inside
me where i yearn
for love
+ it is filled
with moroccan
lanterns
of many colors
+ the wind
is coming through
the open
windows."

belly laughter

i imagine all of us making room in
our bodies for laughter. not the kind
that ridicules, but the kind that heals.
where a bigger picture is given. a
new view. do you remember a time
when your crying turned into laughing
+ anxiety into roaring? didn't it
feel good? maybe because it
opens our windpipes wide to
let the sun in. baking all
our messiness into
marvelous pie.

"i've made some poor choices in my life because someone was baptised right before me & the water was dirty."

* she said while laughing...

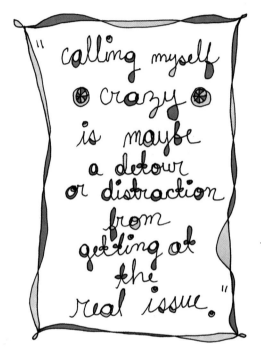

"calling myself ❀ crazy ❀ is maybe a detour or distraction from getting at the real issue."

crazy

if laughter helps our
windpipes to open wide,
then name- calling serves
only to constrict them.
names like crazy only
belittle. they tell us to
not trust what is within
+ scare us into shrinking
back + telling half-truths.

we need our whole
stories to live out
our fullest lives + we
need our whole stories
if others are to also trust us. wisdom comes out of
some intersection of joy + sorrow. no neatness exists.

look at the old woman with her crooked smile +
wrinkled lips. she has one hundred stories to tell you.

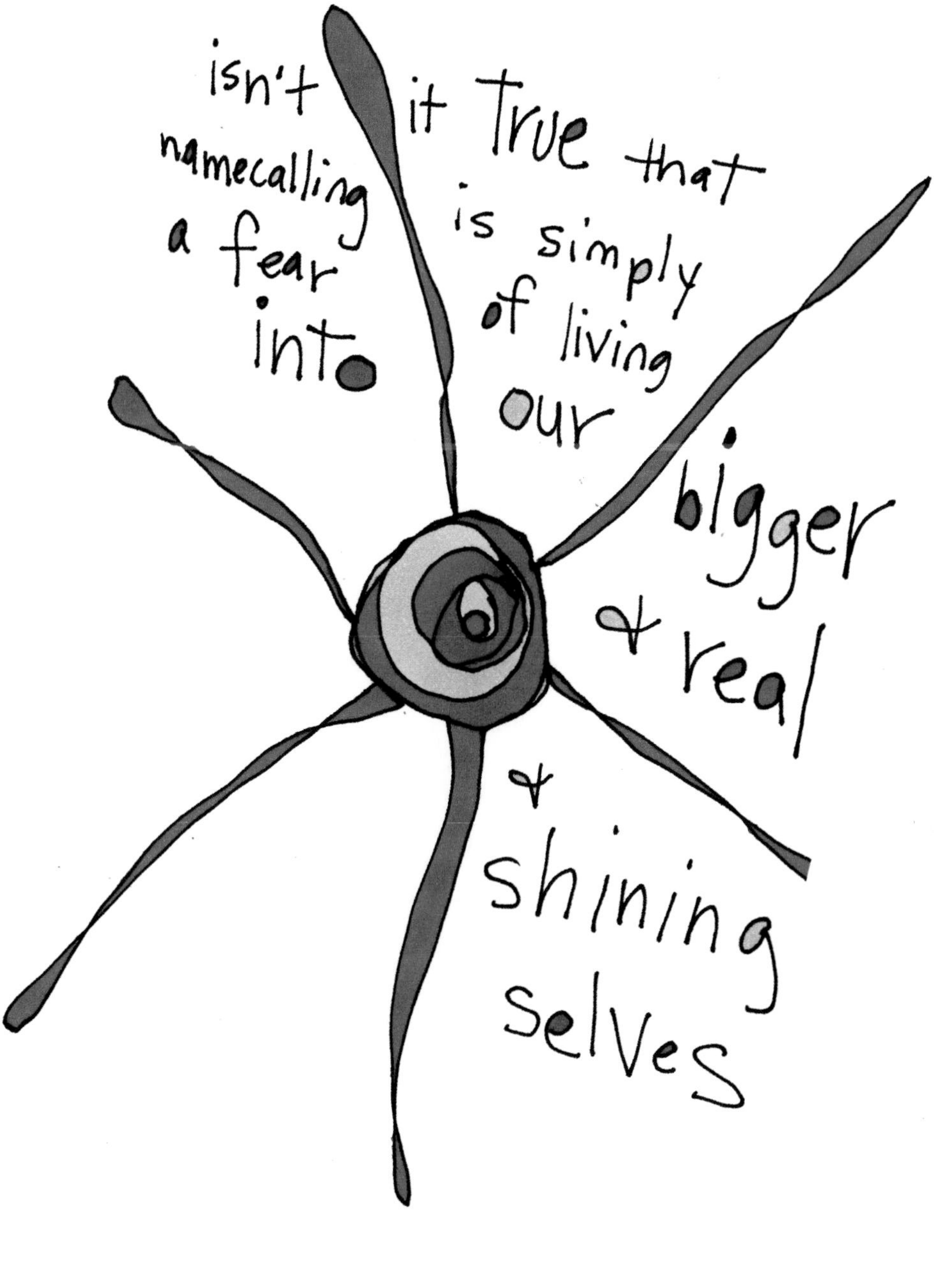

isn't it true that
namecalling is simply
a fear of living
into our
bigger
& real
&
shining
selves

my beauty is still there

pain is hard. feeling bare. weary. we feel our yearns + swallows + breaths as we experience it all + the only power we need to give it is being a witness. in seeing the whole (our pain + our pretty), we can claim these woods as beautiful. there are no conditions for claiming beauty. it is always there in our real story.

"i can feel anything
like...
•sad• •happy•
•worried• •lonely•
•draggy• •funky•
+ •flaw-filled•
⊕
(flaw)
yet i ~~kn~~ know that
my beauty is still
there
anyway + always•"

to life

our real story is also found in our imagination. we knew this as children. we told stories through dolls + action figures + outdoor games + it is still within us.

our imagination can still help give us what we need. we can envision ourselves kicking from a squatting position-dance from the floor when we need to come more into life.

we can close our eyes + lay on a hammock by the ocean when we need rest.

we can lean our ears into the heart of seashells + hear them whisper how greatly we are loved when we need reminding.

we can walk into the real woods of our lives + keep creating.

what do you need right now? what would you like to make?

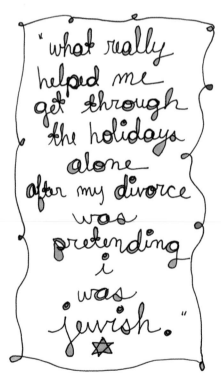

"what really helped me get through the holidays alone after my divorce was pretending i was jewish."

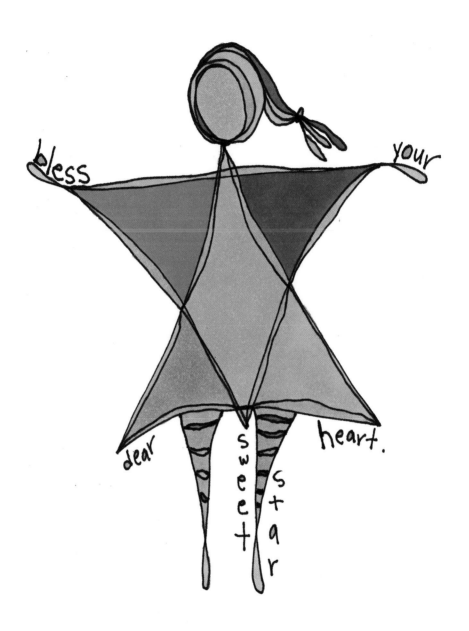

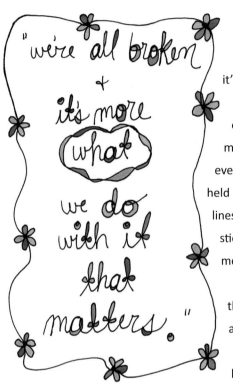

"we're all broken + it's more (what) we do with it that matters."

it's what we do with it

our lives are full of messy material to work with. have you ever dropped a box of spaghetti? held it upside down + then yellow lines dart everywhere? pick up sticks at your feet. monster moans in your mouth.

then comes the confrontation about how to approach it all. leave it + go on the run you've been meaning to take. have the big cry you've been holding in for days. affirm how the pieces of your life are being picked up as you pick them up. ask someone for help at last. pray. breathe.

it's what we do with it that matters. every noodle. to become into me-ing.

doorway conversations

she said this as we approached the door at the end of our first session together.

let's
dive
into
our
delicious
d
e
e
p
s

something deep to learn

my favorite p.o. box exists
in my heart. i love to hear
what piles in. i try to give
special attention to messages i
hear more than once. here are a few of my
own lately. i want to write secret love notes +
leave them in library books. make up lullabies + sing them into a
little recorder. i want to keep telling strangers they are beautiful.
there exists this deep thing. i get into trouble as soon as i stop
paying attention. such messages come in on peacock colored
wings + are meant to be lived. we all feel it. how scary it is to
stretch. to bare teeth + bones into our world. to be here fully.

"i look for something deep to learn when i hear a message more than once because it has always been my goal to be teachable."

"a bee flew into my home & i watched it try to find a way to get out. i had a door wide open & the bee didn't see it ...

wide open doors

could it be that being stuck is about not being present to what we are in? maybe the wide open doors really can be found when we feel all that is real inside us. in opening our eyes wide. accepting our tousled hair. sharing what's in our purses.

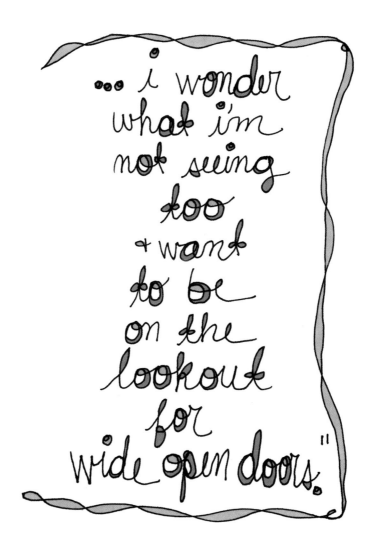

"... i wonder what i'm not seeing too + want to be on the lookout for wide open doors."

listening to our bodies. laughing. loving the old woman. claiming beauty amidst our pain. embracing imagination. caring for spilled noodles. living into how we feel moved to be in this world. especially when we hear our heart calling out more than once. let's put our arms around each other + fly right through.

@
routine  (let's route-in)
summary (sum of me)

on messiness inside

✳ my messiness holds value. it is even embraceable.

✳ sometimes it helps to dump my all into the light.

✳ i am remembering to open windows ⊞ + let the wind into my rooms of honest yearnings.

✳ laughter helps me.

* i am listening to what is real + most important inside.

* my beauty accompanies all my feelings.

* pretending can be my friend.

* anything is possible out of my broken + distressed places.

* we're all in the messiness together. even bees.

two

creation out of chaos*

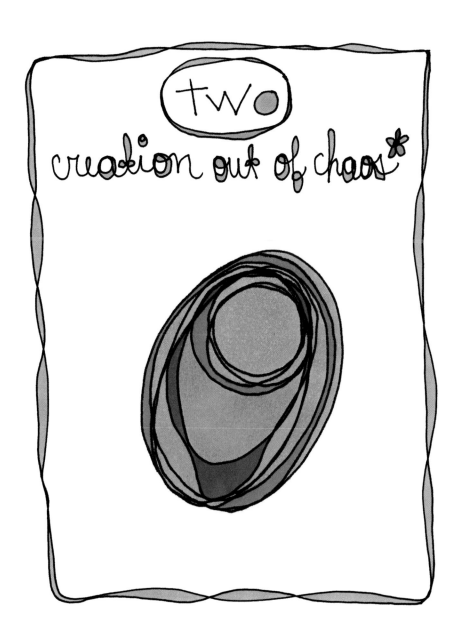

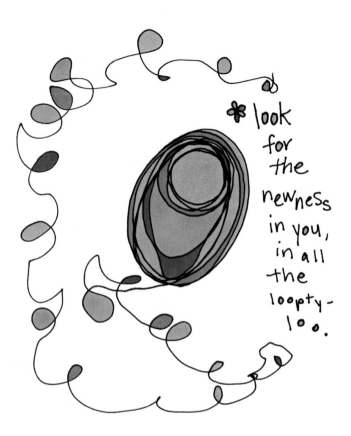

*look
for
the
newness
in you,
in all
the
loopty-
loo.

creation out of chaos

i imagine the visual scene of the making of our world. thunder clasps + waves the size of entire constellations + bright orange fiery crayons drawing trees + mountains all over the earth.

from chaos into creation seems to be the way all new things are made. even now i imagine tonight's soup making. it will need to rumble + bubble + be stirred into a crazed swirl as it prepares to really be something.

"life has become chaotic
for me again
&while
this is difficult,
it helps me
to remember
that creation
came out
of
chaos."

"i've been dancing
with trepidation
because i get
caught up
in the mirror
+ i'd like to
pay attention
to what it feels like
on the inside
+
start dancing
from
there."

dance from the inside

something new always comes
from the inside. babies. a
thought expressed as a light
turned on. steamy sonnets.

none of this is found in
mirrors. or in trying to
measure up. instead, it abides in
bellies. in our minds + marrows.

so i close my eyes to see +
follow my chaos into dance.

dance from the inside ❀

an expedition within

my capacity

distractions often come from outside of us. someone
else's dream. fear. hope.

yet it is only me who can hear my dreams. i have the
only knitting needles to click together the fabric of my
life. it is me who knows how my heart sings for winged
sightings + sublime kisses. i know how i want to draw
near when someone is in pain + see them. i know i
love gentleness + lovely words + water + praise.

only i can make any kind of sense of it + i want to try.

"others have had
high expectations
of me because
my i.q. has been
tested in the
genius range
+
i want to
explore,
instead,
what my capacity
means
to
me."

"im working on trusting what's inside by paying attention to what it feels like when i hear something that is false + something that is true."

trusting what's inside

i tend to feel certain things inside when i hear false messages. when i hear a meanness or something made-up. i feel bored. empty. discouraged. heavy. stopped. ashamed. disturbed. sad.

i feel other things when i hear something true. when i hear something encouraging + solid. i feel light. joy. full. peace. free. when a message is sung in true notes it leaves me feeling good things.

practicing such noticings are powerful. they lead me to trusting what's inside.

can we add this exercise to gym class please?

"i saw families in poverty in haiti + saw them in their beauty + cried myself to sleep + loved them as much as i could + i wonder if i could do something like this for myself too."

something like this

what if we took this inside business really seriously? what if we soaked ourselves silly with compassion for all our hearts go through? what would happen if we saw ourselves in our beauty? what would happen if we listened to our own stories so closely that we cried ourselves to sleep? what would happen if we loved ourselves as much as we could? might we change the whole wide world with such a heart?

i'm practicing loving both the world outside me + within me. ✳

a duet
of heart
+ drum
beats.
*

combining

what hums in our hearts is so quiet + yet sometimes we want to boom
it bigger into a room. speak our needs out loud. say "here i am". pull
out a drum + put our beings into beat. announce our hunger over +
over + not apologize for any of it.

"i have been
combining
saying
what
i need
with the
beating
of
my
drum."

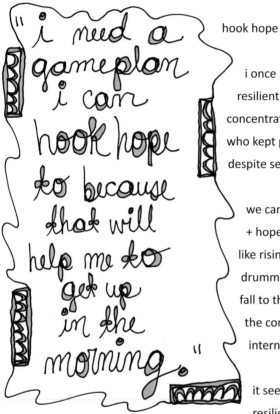

"i need a gameplan i can hook hope to because that will help me to get up in the morning."

hook hope

i once read that the most resilient prisoners in a concentration camp were the ones who kept planning for their futures despite seemingly no hope.

we can all lose track of spark + hope. we don't always feel like rising into a room. into a day. drumming + dancing seem to fall to the bottom of any list. in the commotion + clamor of our internal worlds.

it seems we all need this resilience. we need hope to announce good morning. to say please rise + fry up some eggs. bake banana bread. open the front door + feel the wind in your face. unclench your fists + allow light again into your beautiful palms.

i am noticing recipes that nourish my deeps.

what i can give to myself

i don't want to let others down, but i will + i do. out of my inconsistency. blind spots. clumsiness. noise.

i also can't count on any one person to give me what i need. or know what that is. it is hard to even do this for myself.

often my needs involve the ordinary. add fruit to my cereal. take a walk. turn on music while i clean. remember to look up at the stars.

maybe we can all begin with these things.

" i'm focusing less on what i can't get from others + more on what i can give to myself + i'm beginning with changing my lunches of popcorn to popcorn + progresso soup. "

"instead of
not taking
centering time
because
i am busy,
i am
taking time
to center
because
i am
busy."

busy

so much can pile into a day.
homework. driving children
around. laundry. jobs.

there is this thing i don't
want to miss. it's that our
heart beats in all of it. i need
such sight. i don't want to
live a life of blurry.

let's shine amid our full
plates. take three ten-
minute naps to replenish.
lay out a yoga mat
alongside the sun rising.
write a poem in the middle
of the afternoon.

time spent within,
helps me to bloom.

* good does come

let's look for it

change is some of what piles
into our full lives + how we
see it can make all the
difference. i want to
remember that my
life has purpose +
trust that good will come
as i walk into something new.
let's look for it. a treasure hunt
in our wild woods.

"i trust that good can come with change because i believe that everything has a purpose in the big picture."

"i began to run because i wanted to feel powerful & strong."

powerful + strong

internal work takes
strength. endurance.
chutzpah.

often the
straightforward solution is
the best fitting. if i want to
build strength, i can run.
take vitamins. drink
protein shakes. lift
weights. rest.

then do it all again the
next day.

"i'd make some different choices in my life given what i know now + yet maybe none of that matters because either way, God redeems + makes each day new."

each day new

i can't go back in time with what I know now. regret inhibits. says why bother in the future? it messes with my sense of worth.

i want to lay regret to rest. it drains my strength.
i want to lay my hand on my heart + make humming sounds over such aching.
i want to learn something new. i need to be encouraged that each day is fresh. i want to walk into it with a handful of sunlit dandelions.

i stand in a new day.

"i began to notice how some circles of people in my life weren't life-giving for me..."

get out in order to get in

there is much indeed to get out of in order to get in. out of false messages about ourselves + regret. out of circles of people who don't honor us. out of all that holds us down + keeps us from soaring.

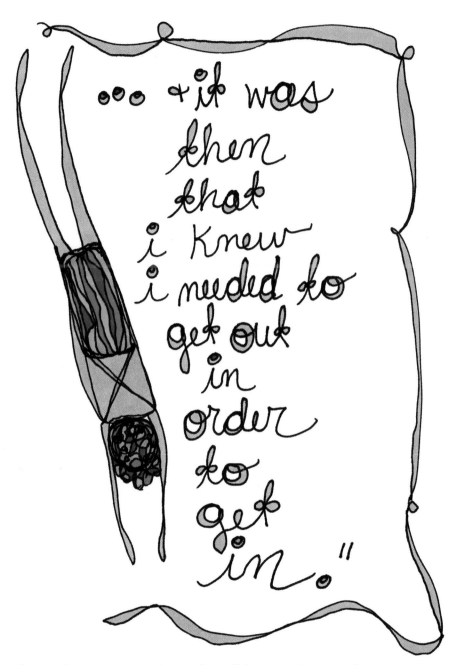

... +it was then that i knew i needed to get out in order to get in."

let's instead turn in. into our dreams. into all that's true. love ourselves as much as we can. hope. give ourselves what we need. shine. look for the good. build strength + rise into a new day.

@
routine (let's route-in)
summary (sum of me)

on creation out of chaos

* new life springs
from me. even out
of chaos.

* i am trusting
what is inside.

* i am exploring what
my capacity means
to me.

* loving me as much
as i can is my work.

* i am creating:
  °hopeful plans
  °nourishing recipes
  °centering time.

* good does come.
  so does strength.
  everyday is new.
  i drum it.

* i am getting in
  &
  dancing from
  ~there~

"what i really
want is
to wake up
in the morning
+ be happy
+ enjoy
the
world
we
have."

wake up

i am here. alive. now.
i want to be awake. i
want to hear the snow
crunch as i walk. smell
pages of a new book.
taste every drippy bite of
a peach. hug loved ones.
tight. cry at the sight of a
newborn. remain in awe
of the lilac tree every
spring. be surprised
that the moon looks
so big. that a deer is
in my yard. that a heart
is in my chest. grow into
the wise toddler where
everything is wonder.
astonishment. gift.

awakenings are powerful.

i want to let more love in ❀ even in my dreams. ♡

in my dreams

i want to be attentive to the day
+ also the night of me. i want to
be present to the language of
my dreams. to what i'm feeling.
needing. being. we are all
brilliant in this place. worthy of
leaning into + listening. let's run
to it like a wide-open field of
daisies. i will look for you there.

"i began bringing
the lost girl
in my dreams
nourishment
+ blankets
+ i spoke with her
+ now
she is off
to great
adventures."

more than anything

what do you want to wake
up to? what would you love
in your day if you would dare
speak it? gently lay down any
words of can't + unrealistic +
consider for a moment words
of yes + miracle. let pictures
unfold like they do in your
dreams. freely. you don't need
to make complicated plans. just
breathe beside them. see them.
say hello.

what do i want to wake up to?

"more than anything, i want to wake up in the morning + shuffle downstairs to enjoy a leisurely breakfast + settle into work at my desk + create adventures + dramas + know that people await my stories eagerly + do this knowing in my heart that there is someone out there missing me."

"let's flush all our shoulds down the toilet with the dead goldfish. (bless those finned friends)"

shoulds

i want to follow my heart
+ let go of thoughts that
limit me. i want to turn
my gaze to the ocean.
so much lives there.
i remember gasping
the first time i saw sea
dragons. they look like
they are from fairy tales
but they are real. we can
be like this ocean + hold
endless possibility. we too
are made mostly of water.

today i will follow my heart.

what if we *all* looked to see *all* the amazing gifts forming inside us?

the waiting room

it is hard to wait. most of us prefer a delivery
of right away. yet most physical spaces tell us
otherwise. the room before the room. waiting to
see the doctor. dentist. principal. what if we were
awake to a sense of purpose even here? what if
we were to bring a journal + write about what
we are experiencing inside? what if we talked
to someone new beside us? what if we saw this
place as part of our appointment? what if we
woke up everywhere?

"it's hard to be in the waiting room of my life but i am finding gifts forming here of patience + wisdom."

"i have been trying to respond with greater freedom to what i need + so when i hosted thanksgiving last year, i let go of having to use the china dishes."

greater freedom

we become keenly aware of our needs as we wake up to the world inside + outside of us. this allows for greater freedom in how we step forward. we can see everything as gift. a window to be amazed. we can breathe into what we would like our day to become. into what we would like our very lives to become. follow our hearts + even savor the waiting.

i am moving into greater freedom.

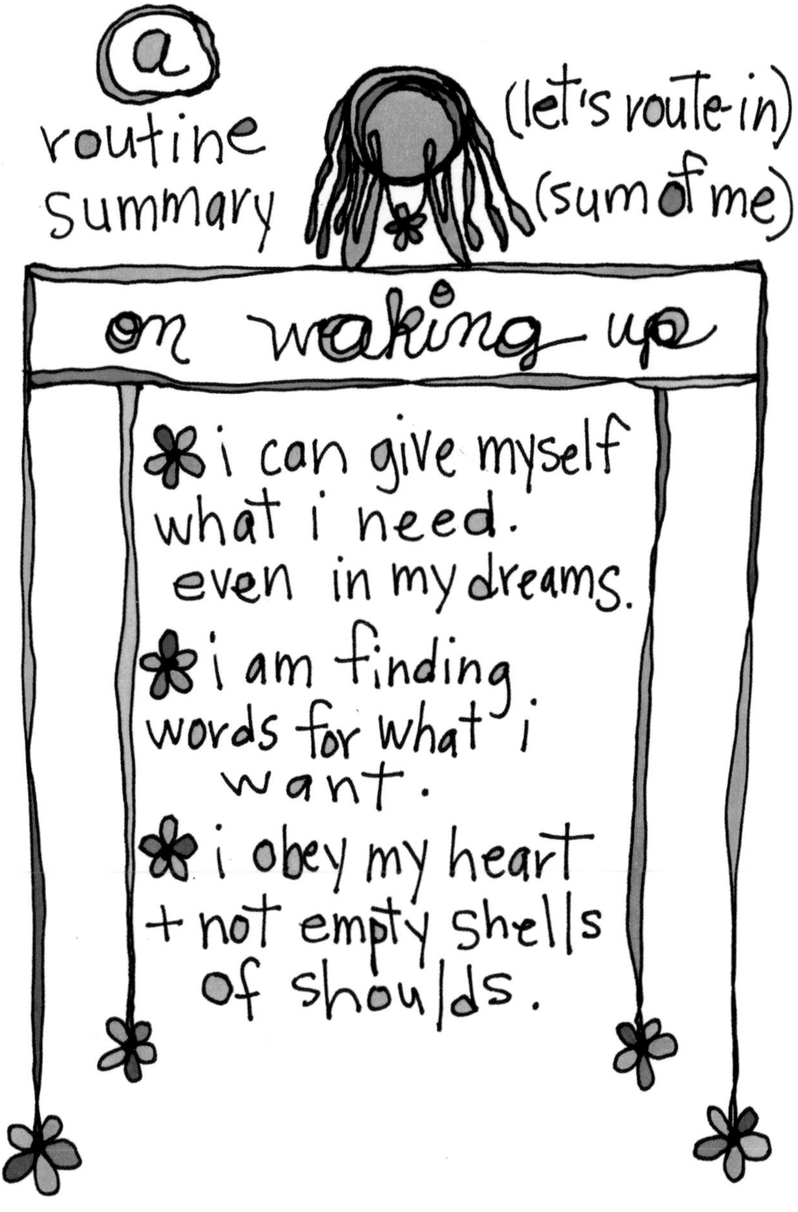

@

routine
summary

(let's route-in)
(sum of me)

on waking up

✲ i can give myself
what i need.
even in my dreams.

✲ i am finding
words for what i
want.

✲ i obey my heart
+ not empty shells
of shoulds.

* gifts are forming in my rooms. even the rooms that are hard to be in.

* greater freedom is mine for the taking. the china dishes understand.

* i am leaning into happiness + enjoying our world.

* lights are on + i am waking up.

four

room for flowers*

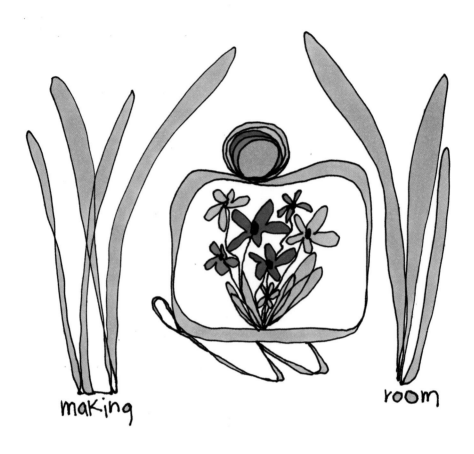

making   room

room for flowers

it's time to prune. to let go of
what's withered + water the rest.
we can make room. expansive.
indulgent. delectable room.

"i'm praying for weeds to come out of my heart + make room for flowers."

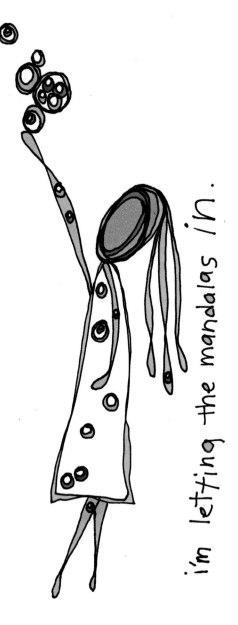

mandalas

maybe we
begin with making
room
for mandalas.
beautiful
pictures.
circling into
wholeness.
dear mandala maker,
please pour me a cup
to overflowing.

i'm letting the mandalas in.

"i saw a group
of monks
create mandalas
out of sand
+ pour them
into a river
to spread
peace
+ i would like
this to pour
into me
too."

"i am not going to be so fixed on my plan because along the way, there may be something fascinating like a deer or a bunny or a sale."

plans

our world is full of surprises. one day i am on our way to the grocery store. plans only to pick-up the regular menu of pasta + peas. but now the unexpected. there is a lemonade stand alongside the road. to stop or not to stop. if i am conscious of wanting to make room for flowers then my decision is clear. i will stop + i will start receiving all that this life wants to give me.

i want a life of fascination.

"i am creating more happiness by adding color to my walls."

creating more happiness

i want to be an active participant in this glorious life + keep trying out different things to discover what beckons my heart to sing.

plant tulip bulbs. serve at a soup kitchen. color my walls. pay attention to the music that i make + join my song with yours.

combine our joy so big that even the stars can hear us.

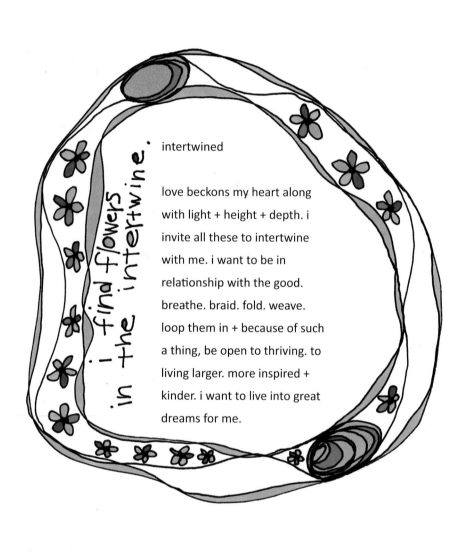

i find flowers in the intertwine.

intertwined

love beckons my heart along with light + height + depth. i invite all these to intertwine with me. i want to be in relationship with the good. breathe. braid. fold. weave. loop them in + because of such a thing, be open to thriving. to living larger. more inspired + kinder. i want to live into great dreams for me.

"it helps me
to thrive
when
my mind
&
God's
are
intertwined."

plant our crop

not every flower will bloom even
if i make room. if we want to live
into great dreams we must kneel +
get our knees dirty. create from the
ground up. plant. plant. plant. pour
everything of us in + know a response
to our work will be uneven. we don't
get the job we were hoping for or in
the timing we thought it would be.
we don't like the class we signed up
for but made a new friend. someone
hurts us + at another time someone
loves us back. let's gather up our
dirty knees + kiss them silly + then
kneel back down + keep planting.

"my old boyfriend cheated on me + i'm afraid to trust the one i'm with now. i want to be like the farmer who plants her crop to succeed, even though not every year is fruitful, + love anyway."

"i am preparing for the next phase of my life by taking more bubble baths, painting my nails, + journaling + i call this marinating."

marinating

there exists this thing where i need to be constantly working in the field of my life. planting + reaping. a posture of dirty kneeing. then there are times when i need special attention. something important is approaching + extra loving care is in order.

my posture changes. i stand up + reach for an ice cream cone. put on flower leggings. lay down at the water's edge + listen before the interview. the doctor's appointment. the day. i marinate for a while + do this because it might just change everything.

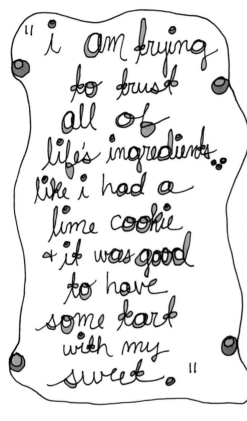

"i am trying to trust all of life's ingredients... like i had a lime cookie + it was good to have some tart with my sweet."

all of life's ingredients

i want to open to all the
ingredients that will make this
life the richest. i want to greet
the path that had extra hills
with gratitude for the strength
it built into me. i want to feel
the pain in good-bye so i can
more fully feel the joy in hello.
i want to welcome the sugar
+ the lime of the cookie to
my table so i can awaken my
senses more completely.

i want to welcome the fullness
of you to my table + the fullness
of me + trust all of it.

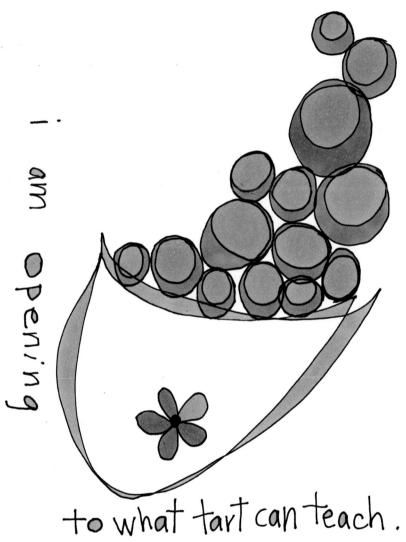

i am opening

to what tart can teach.

"despite the acidic soil in my garden, i noticed there were places i could still grow things + that gave me hope for my own life."

places i could still grow things

we are made for growing. new hair replaces old. nails rise. even bones keep changing. cells renew tissue. our bodies work to put ourselves back together again after a break. we move in the direction of newness. it is our nature.

this is good news because sometimes i break + i'm not always in the mood to step forward. to keep my chin up + grin. yet, in my truest of trues, i don't want to sink. i don't want to stay in a sunken place. i need to know that something new is still possible for me. i need to know that something is still possible for all of us.

authentic

come as you are. bring your
true nature. your continually
renewing bones. what ever
words are dwelling in your
heart at this moment. come.
you do not need to appear
fancy at all. wear what
pleases you. allow your
heart to love what you love.
you do not need to make
everyone laugh in the room
+ you do not need to eclipse
into a corner. you only need to
be here. that is enough.

our world needs the
present + authentic you.
maybe that is the real
substance of fancy. the true
dazzle. the place where light
breaks free.

i am worth something.

"i don't see myself
as knockout gorgeous
or wildly talented
but want
to find
good people
&
feel
complete,
authentic,
&
worth
something."

"i found something
lovely
to touch
my neck
because
the grief
inside
me
needed
fresh
air."

found something lovely

there is this thing that happens
when i become increasingly present
+ authentic. when i am paying
attention to what is real. i begin to
hear what is going on with me more
deeply. the stories of my gladness.
the pangs of my suffering. the pulls +
tugs + calls of my dreams + hopes +
all that i house within me.

i want to respond generously. send
in love letters. ice cream cones.
harp music. sometimes i need a
whole day of extra love. dive into
a high rise of magazines. movies.
mystery novels.

my very skin tells me that this is
the thing to do. this brilliant fabric
woven with pores. open to receive.
to breathe in all i need.

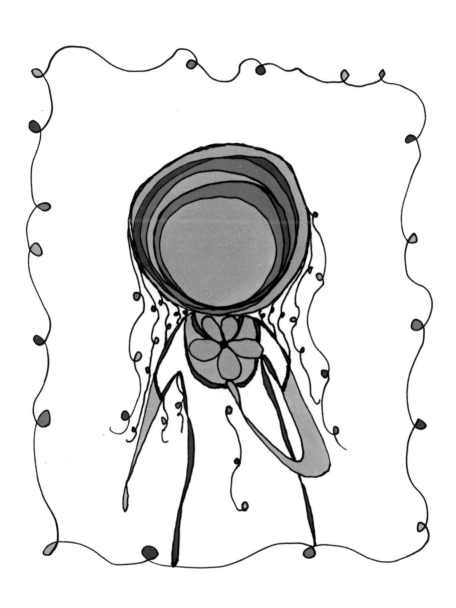

choosing clothing

much gets set in motion when i
really hear myself. including an
evolution of my closet. or maybe it's
a revolution. an unrest for all that
doesn't fit. for the uncomfortable.
for the fashion of someone else.
there comes this time when i want
my clothes to match me. i want
leggings like little girls have. with
stripes + flowers. because i adore
such freedom of being. i want to draw
faces + simple houses with fabric
markers on skirts. because i love to
draw. in winter i want to put on warm
layers + relate to each one. say good
morning to the purple + i love you to
the orange. because i don't want to
be removed from any of it. from any
of me. i don't want to miss this chance
to really dress up.

"i find that i am
choosing
clothing
i like
for me
more consciously
as i begin
to listen
to my
feelings
more
closely."

"i want to love my body + have been shielding it to avoid being hurt— yet a shield lets nothing pass in either direction...

a softer boundary

i want my clothes to delight me. lift + light me + somehow be like me. i want to keep paying attention this. to asking myself if a scarf feels lovely against my skin. do my shoes make walking lighter? prettier? for me.

"... & so i think it would be better to consider a softer boundary like my purple poncho."

i also want to consider my relationships. are my clothes soft? noticeable? how do i make room for others? when do i put on wool? blend in? keep out? what is this letter i write to other people on my body? what is yours? what would you like to say?

"signing up for a computer dating service is next on my list but all i really feel like doing is finding a cat + buying a deep, bright, pink mouse for my computer."

all i really feel like doing

i want to engage in what i love. turn on the music that makes me sail + swoon. create a happy bag filled with delights. for markers + bubble gum + fun reads + have it be just as important as my purse. notice the sky rise with bright pink + walk out my front door to greet it. i don't want to be so serious all the time. i don't want to forget to enjoy my life.

"ive shown up for others for so long + i'm finally listening to my own wants too + it felt good to get a couple things ive always wanted... a box of costumes + a tea set"

listening to my own wants too

i am laying out a path before you. it is made up of flat yellow stones. these stones are framed by grass with little flowers at the tip of each blade. this is your walk up to a cottage. i greet you at the door. you are welcome here. safe. comfortable. loved.

it is here that we know how beautifully you have given to others + it is also time to give to you + enjoy every minute.

what does your heart desire? what can you give yourself? paper dolls? yarn? a music box? new nail polish? a walk? a candle lit room? it is all yours for the taking. please trust the pretty stones + flowers that have led you to this place.

i can have more opinions

i find myself astounded with what
arrives when i make room for
beauty. a handful of dandelions. a
selection of gold + silver crayons.
bright banana taffy.

i also see that it is me
who is all this goodness.
my thoughts are like the
gathered flowers i can offer
others. my heart is like the
glittery sticks i create with.
my very life is the gift of
delightful taffy to delight in.

there is this thing that keeps
on growing inside if we let it.

"i am gathering courage in believing i can have more opinions about politics + life, like i saw rosie o'donnell do on the t.v. show 'the view'."

i am gathering all the courage i need.

wonderment wrapping

awake to wonderment

i find beauty when i have my eyes open for it + such riches do come when i open myself. i want to be awake for the whole transaction. i don't want to sleep any of it away. so i will lie under the christmas tree. paint the sunset. taste the food i eat. the pear. the plum.

this is the lightweight i wish to carry. what i want my belly to be filled with + spill over with symptoms of awe + wonderment.

"i caught a
glimpse
of our daughter
laying under the
twinkling lights of
the Christmas tree
+ now i too
want to be
awake
to
wonderment."

"i'm beginning
to accept
there's something
beautiful in being
imperfectly me,
like the woman
who carried
water
in a
cracked pot
everyday. . .

imperfectly me

there are days of flatness. no flow. it seems everything is an effort. my words come out in a way that would award red pen marks all over a page from an english teacher. my coffee spills. no outfit looks appealing in my closet. might as well stay in my pajamas.

...+ because the water was leaking, she created a path of flowers everywhere she walked."

i also know i need to water myself steadily nonetheless. can you hear the great waterfalls of the world? pouring constant love letters + lullabies + life into us? maybe i need to keep my arms open. at some point there will be flowers. it seems to be the law of the heart.

"i plan to create a necklace of a woman's body + voice + i will make her voice the gems."

her voice

we are all treasure chests with hearts in the middle + we get to make room for what really belongs inside. water. mandalas. surprises. creating. intertwining with the good. planting. marinating. being our fullest. growing. being authentic. receiving. dressing up. being deliberate with what we keep in + what we keep out. engaging in what we love. listening to what we want. trusting our thoughts. waking up to wonderment. pressing imperfectly on.

gems will appear. voices heard. even sung. they have been there all along. needing to be mined + they are all mine + they are all yours.

@

routine summary (let's route-in) (sum of me)

on room for flowers

* i pray for room for flowers +mandalas+fresh air inside.
* my path allows me bunnies.
* i am consciously choosing my clothing + coloring walls.
* intertwining goodness helps me. so does purple ponchos.
* fruit or no fruit, i am loving anyway.
* there is always a place for growth, even with the tart.

* i am doing more of what i feel like doing + even leaving flowers on my path.
* i am gathering courage + showing up.
* awakening to wonderment is magical.
* i am worth so much something that my every word is a gem.
* i am marinating me.

"i used to be in a choir where we'd hold hands in a circle + listen for each other's notes + contribute our own..."

hold hands

sometimes it takes only one friend or experience to unlock something powerful within. the kind who remind us of how essential it is to be ourselves in the world. who invite us to be distinct. who really know how to hold our hands. who can celebrate how our notes come together + create new life. like how two sticks make fire.

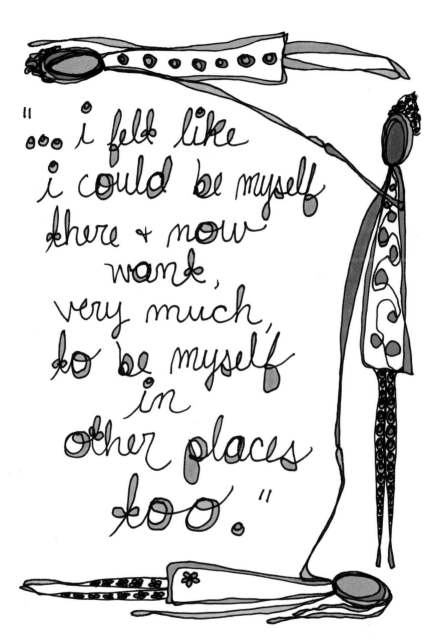

"... i felt like i could be myself there + now want, very much, to be myself in other places too."

i am warmed by such a flame. i can eat. dance. howl if i want to. be seen on my island. being both myself + in this kind of relationship frees me. i can hear sparks inside even now if i get quiet enough.

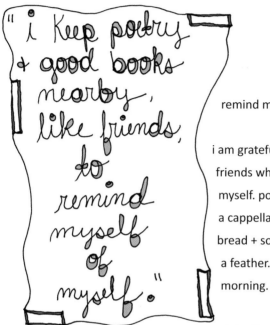

"i keep poetry + good books nearby, like friends, to remind myself of myself."

remind myself of myself

i am grateful for the gamut of friends who remind myself of myself. poetry books. singing a cappella. deer. trees. stones. bread + soup. pretty buttons. a feather. water. solitude. morning.

i don't want to miss anyone of them. because i don't want to miss the chance to stretch further into being true + i don't want to miss the chance to thank them all.

*i love these words
on pages
that
find
+
friend
me.

sitting with my feelings

calling all travelers. those with arms open wide + chests revealed. brave + hungry to live honesty + deeply. to feel what you feel. to know the stories residing in the living room of your hearts. who wish for tea parties in such a place. where there is no such thing as telling each other about what is right or what should happen. come along with me.

let's sit together with our feelings. in the open + breathe + trust that this is getting us somewhere + we don't need to go anywhere else to find it.

"sitting with my feelings helps move me to a different plane + i'd like to have likewise companions on board."

> "i have been
> thinking
> that my
> love of
> goodness
> +how much
> i like hoss
> from bonanza
> has something
> to do with
> who i am."

i like hoss

who are famous people you feel
drawn to? maybe even dream
of? an actor? musician? writer?
artist? athlete? humanitarian?
what is the gift you are being
given? what are you hearing?
what does their presence have
to do with who you are?

julia roberts + pippi
longstocking have been a
couple of those people for me.
as different as they may appear
to be, they are both friends who
remind me to keep living fuller. to
laugh larger. to be in my beauty +
charge forward into dreams + be
myself through it all.

i don't want to close off from any
gates of friendship. our world is so
big + bursting with life to love + be
loved by.

mi love & goodness.

not so alone after all

great company can come from
life that is big + mysterious.
bodies of water. constellations.
butterfly migrations.

it can feel even more
intimate when the
arrival is a surprise. a
sudden wind. a relevant
song played on the radio.
the lights turn on.

this is where we find
ourselves in this very
big world + maybe not so
alone after all.

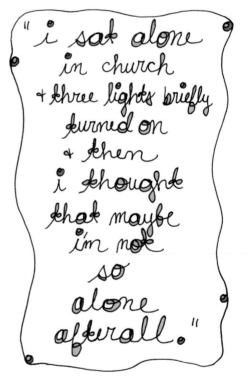

"i sat alone
in church
+ three lights briefly
turned on
+ then
i thought
that maybe
i'm not
so
alone
afterall."

t she sat here for a while.

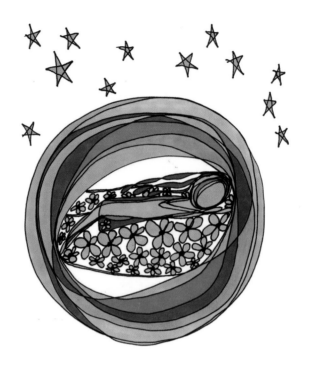

half-asleep

here rest encounters that can
be long lasting. being in a state
of half-asleep is like stepping
into a magical forest. intuitive
knowings bud. a whisper is
heard from a loved one who has
passed. a new poem is written. a
whole song composed.

sometimes it is when we finally
rest that we find that our hands
are held.

"one night,
before my mom died,
she hugged me
when i was
half-asleep
+ now
i feel
that will
hold me
the rest
of my life."

" my mom's house is a mess + she's been expecting a lot from me + i told my brother she's been pressing my buttons + he said if our mom wants to press buttons, she should try the vacuum. "

press buttons

not everyone holds ease for us. we don't always want to hold hands. especially when we experience our buttons being pressed. pulled. prodded.

then we find ourselves in need of something more. a nurturing friend to close the day with. a bath. tea. new boundaries. a rigorous walk. a gentle breath + releasing it all. into crying. into laughter. into whispering on our knees.

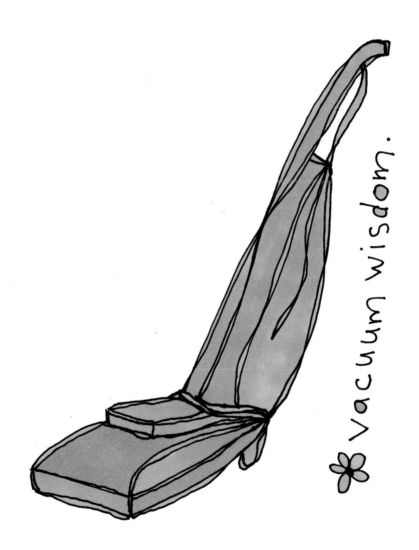

❀ Vacuum wisdom.

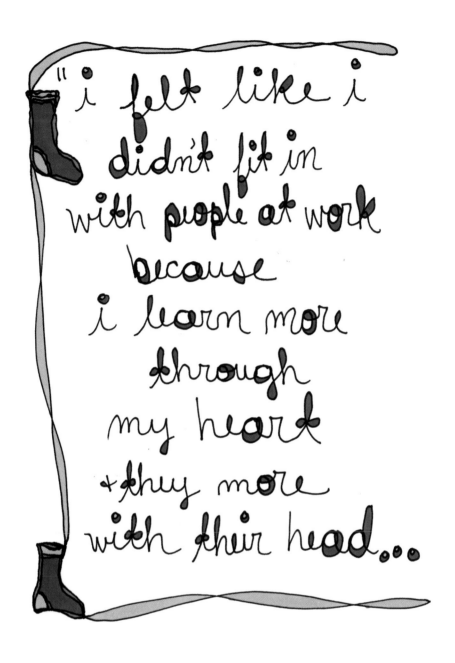

"i felt like i didn't fit in with people at work because i learn more through my heart + they more with their head...

fitting in

i don't want to fit in. i want to stand out + shine with people who are being their real selves + who invite me to be my real self. i want us all to bring our true instruments into the room.

... then i got busy rounding up christmas stockings + gave them out to homeless people + that helped me to consider that being different was maybe ok. "

can you just see us now? harmonicas. tambourines. ukuleles. bongos. banjos. triangles + pots + pans. a line of beauties marching the whole distance of the milky way.

accepting

the good thing.

to accept the good thing

as i have made room within for
mandalas + all things lovely, i
have found a room outside of
me too. i want it filled with
goodness. with people who
are kind. gentle. brave. sincere.
plump of heart. imperfectly
wonderful.

we can all make such choices
consciously + with great hope,
because the direction love
always wants to go is in.

"after a bumpy
romantic life,
i have finally met
a kind man...
+ now i'm
hoping
i'll continue
to accept
the good thing
when it comes along
in other things
too."

"i was going to see a doctor for a prescription because i was feeling blue but instead, i called my mother."

such a phone

i am no wiring wizard. but i am painting buzzing lines of my favorite colors. connecting my inner + outer rooms. mostly orange + green lines today. some turquoise too. they are wide enough to be sturdy + spirally enough to be soulful. there is white space in between each one for pause. breathing space. savoring.

this whole medley is made for being with those i love. who help me bloom + i wish bloom back.

i wonder what such a phone's ringing would sound like? daffodils rising? the moon dreaming?

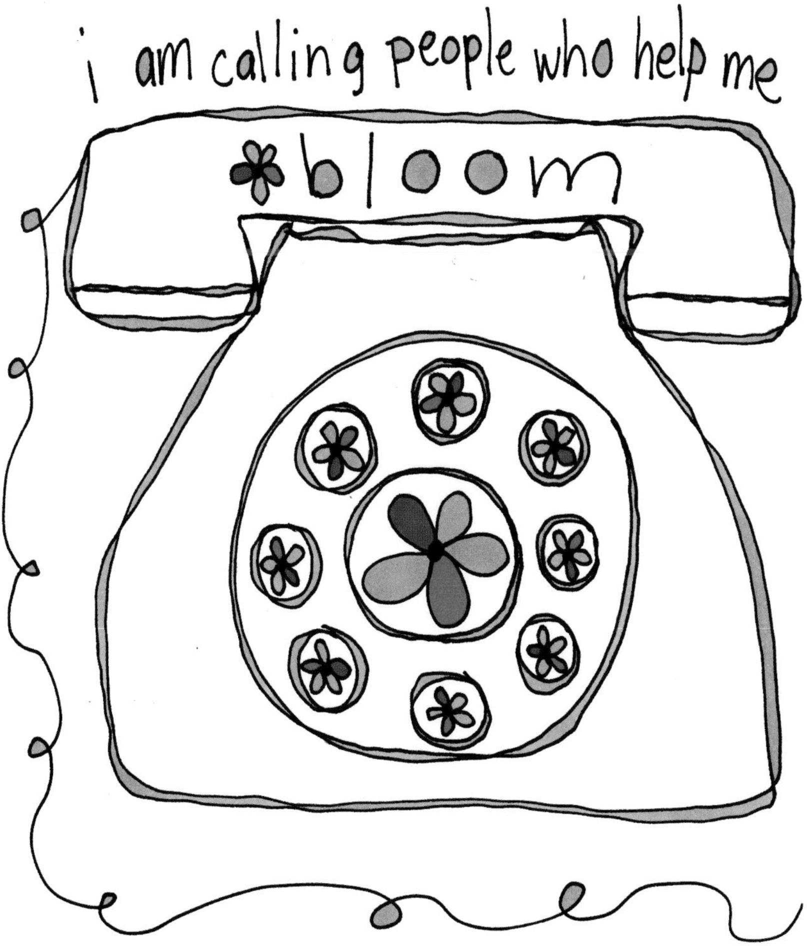
i am calling people who help me
bloom

to find company

it was time for a mid-day break
+ the woods looked enticing +
the sun, softly shining. i found +
followed a path toward a field of
cattails. i walked in far enough until
i was surrounded. they sounded
like musical instruments
as they swayed in the
wind. i slowly moved my
body with them + breathed in
the moment.

then. a little green bird landed
right in front of me. time
ceased for a second. then. by +
by we had to return to where
we came from. it was time to
fly. time to walk.

i count this feathered friend
as one of my best.

"i am trying to take more walks + it helped me to find company i could feed on my path in the form of a duckling."

> "i sense our purpose is to be connected in love + so i want to work through all my barriers."

connected in love

pain does come. someone dies. another speaks a hurtful word. doesn't call. doesn't seem to care anymore. we then walk a thousand days with sorrow + the thought of lifting our head feels as difficult as achieving a back handspring.

we don't want to be hurt anymore. don't think we can bare it + so we change bare into barriers + harden. hide. hush our hearts.

still, love persists. if connection is part of my purpose, i want to heal. i want to open up to this tender work. i want to respond + say i love you. over + over.

i connect to my purpose when i connect in love.

> " sometimes all we ever really need from each other is to cluck sympathetically. "

cluck sympathetically

sometimes our world only requires of us a simple response. we are relieved of having to come up with crafty advice or charming retorts in order to connect. instead, all we need offer is an utterance. breath. sigh. cluck.

we know this exchange from watching the snowfall. the steam rise from our coffee + tea. from taking in the air of cinnamon at the bakery. we know this from our exhale that follows all of this.

maybe this teaches us what all our relationships need. maybe we could open our hearts wide enough to be beside each other in awe. most surely we are as stunning as the snow + steam + cinnamon.

i love to cluck sympathetically.

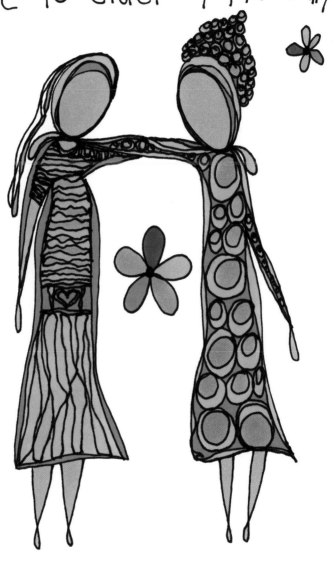

"i have read wuthering heights every year since i was little + have been struck how the free spirit + serious character never married..."

parts of myself

i have a little secret. i would like to be a matchmaker + sit at a quaint table amidst a field of sunflowers + offer a pitcher of lemonade + plate of cookies. people looking for love would come + they would take me on a tour of their heart. then they would be matched with someone to love every part, including the terrain of the messy + tender.

"...i wonder how these two parts of myself could be more integrated, fall in love, & marry."

✳ ✳ ✳

then we would do this for ourselves + tour within. introduce every part. beckon each one out of hiding. listen to how one story relates to the next + the next. trust we have done the best we could with what we knew at the time. learn from it all. allow our internal faces/roles/spaces to be friends. to make peace. hold hands + fall madly in love.

love is my gravity

i want to feel the weight of love. hold hands with it. sit with how it all feels.

i want to be grateful for the gamut of connections. with others + with myself. for poetry books + morning. for animals. for famous people. for the mysteriousness of constellations + sudden light. for encounters when i am half-asleep.

i want to let go of fitting in + stand out + shine. i want to accept good people into my life. who help me bloom + who i wish bloom back.

mostly i want to connect in love + breathe + sigh + cluck.

@

routine
summary

(let's route-in)
(sum of me)

on hold hands

* i want to be myself everywhere.
* good books remind myself of myself.
* i am choosing friends who sit with their feelings.
* the goodness i am drawn to in others reflects back the goodness i have in me.
* i am not alone.

* i rest in what holds me.
even vacuums + ducklings.
* being different
    gifts the world.
* i am letting in kindness
+ people who help me bloom.
* clucking sympathetically
        h e l p s .
* connecting in love
connects me to my purpose.
it is my gravity.
* i am integrating
    all of me,

six

a clear stream running

"i can see a clear stream running. it is the time when the bottom is not stirred up. this was when the pioneers saw it as a safe time to cross over. i think now is the time for me to do the same."

a clear stream running

there is a timing about stepping into the next thing. we cannot rush our river.

i want to have my shining shoes ready + muscles stretched long enough for leaping. i want to have all my beloved messiness + glorious flowers + weight of love with me.

i know this much. i want to learn from all that is green + keep sprouting + springing + becoming + flourish.

i am ready.

all is clear + it's time
for me to cross over.

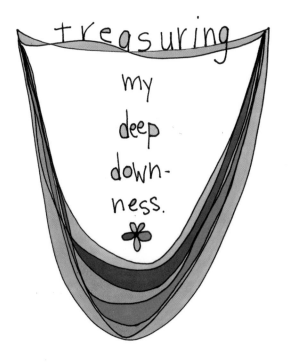

treasuring my deep down-ness.

follow my intuition + be myself

the woods used to be my backyard. often
i would walk in them + go where i felt like
going. always new discoveries were found.
an injured bird to scoop up. a fort to build. a
new favorite stone. i trusted my own leading.
my stopping. starting. breathing.

such a path paved long ago is still within me
+ raw trust, still my task.

"i get afraid of what
i will find by
following my
intuition
+ being myself
but i know,
deep down,
that what i will find
if i don't follow
my intuition
+ be myself
will be far
more
frightening."

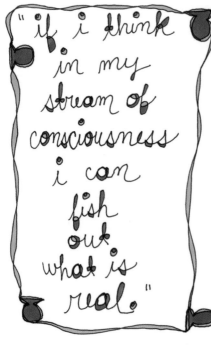

"if i think in my stream of consciousness i can fish out what is real."

stream of consciousness

streams of thought rush in as i lay down to sleep. a telephone conversation. someone i need to call. what i still need to do. laundry. bills. bustle.

then something else. a new thought comes in. a peace. saying "all in good time" + i recognize this thought as right + real + i needed the whole stream to get there.

there lives this great aquarium within us all. teeming with plenty.

i'm going fishin'!

it is okay to be

i need to pay attention to my emotional life if i am to keep moving. as soon as i block this process, i get stuck. if i say "don't be angry", i am angrier or "don't be afraid", i am more scared. it seems they request from me my bravest self. my curiosity. they like it better when i say "i hear you. you are welcome. stay as long as you need to. get cozy in the purple chair + when you are ready, teach me about you. about what brought you here."

ultimately those feelings do transform + make something new. because that is what happens when we let love be the wild thing it is. when we let it loose to do its thing.

"i was afraid of going
to the dentist
+ even though
i needed to go,
i knew what i needed
most was to
feel my feelings...
soon after i told
myself it is ok to
be afraid,
i felt my
courage rising.

"i don't want
to walk
like fear does
(like a rabbit)
but instead,
tall,
like
a
lion."

walking tall

what if we walked tall as we
crossed over + continued on with
such a posture? like the wolf. like
the lion.

what knowledge do they hold in
their spirited beings that allow
for straight spines + steady gazes?
does such strength come from
knowing they belong? from
having a voice? from knowing they
are beautiful + capable? do they pass
on such a code through their bones
from generation to generation?

if any of this is true, then let's
cultivate these same things + press
on + pass them along to all we love.

you are invited to walk tall. *

i am taking in bright faces.

returning to what is lovely

i want to drench myself in the goodness of this world.
plunge my face into a barrel of apples + capture
crispness. flap my angel wings in snow from side to side
+ laugh into the night.

this is important work. since joy builds upon joy.

"i am returning
to what is
lovely,....
like when i am
teaching,
i'm focusing less
on the one
disgruntled student
+ more
on the many
bright
faces. "

i could be the river

i could be the firefly. the one
who keeps buzzing. is full of
life + spark + wing.

i could be the
gazelle. navigate wild
terrain. bound + leap.
purposefully.

i could be the river + not
hold on to anything. allow
circumstances to be what
they are + not be held
hostage. instead, create
the routes i need + enjoy
the sound i make as i go.

"i feel like sandbags
keep being thrown
at me
+ sinking me
down
+ yet,
maybe
i could change
this picture
+ i could be
the river
+ create new routes."

resting in new routes.

"it feels better to be creating my life instead of sitting around + wondering what's going to happen next."

creating my life

we hold this untamed thing within of longing. its power stretches deep + wide. our hearts rumble as we await our desires being met. as if the air is freezing, we can see our breath as we pace at the gate.

certainly, there is a time for waiting + a time for crossing over. if you can see your breath, don't wait to hear if you got into cooking school. take out the cherries + oranges now + make that jubilee. call the person you love. read the book you've set down. let out your song + hear it echo all the way down the river.

creating my life.

best choices

there is much in life to capture our
attention. piles of dishes + laundry
+ the smell of cookies baking +
apple cider simmering + stepping
out the front door to look
at the sunset. the moon +
a million stars.

yet i would walk away from
all of it. i would cross over
anything. rivers. mountains.
worlds. to hear "i love you".

"i don't want to
make good choices
but
best choices...
like walking away
from making the bed
+ saying
yes
when my daughter asks
will you
dance with me?"

i am saying yes to all that's best.

"i don't feel anxiety in my stomach anymore since i started filling it with things that are good for me."

good fillings

there is all kinds of talk these days about smoothies. pull together a mishmash of healthy ingredients + spin them around in a blender with ice. bananas + apple juice + yogurt + spinach. cantaloupe + honeydew + almond milk + mint.

they are drank before leaving for work in the morning. before school. before the sun rises. graduation party menus are centered around them.

i wonder what my fridge would look like if i shopped with these tall orders in mind + i wonder how my body would feel if i gave such thoughtful gifts.

i want to fill
myself with goodness.

i am gaining momentum.

momentum

i was talking with someone who had bicycled across the united states. he said that going uphill began with a decision in his mind. he would pedal a little way up + then rest + pedal a little more + rest a little more. then somehow he could go further with each time.

finally all this moved from his mind into his body + he was able to go even further + all the way to the top.

he added that momentum is not about going down hills. it is about going up.

"there is
great power
in getting going
with something
because
momentum begins...
like
once a train
gains speed,
it is almost
impossible
to stop."

"i'm thinking about going back to school but it might only be a pipe dream... then again, pipes are also in places i like, like in organs."

pipe dreams

our very life begins with little bits at a time. one word. "mama." "dada." then we go a little further + string two + three words together. "i want ball" + then paragraphs + then whole lives.

i want to be aware of how powerful my words are. of how i can play with them + create. the sky is indeed the limit. although today i might take out the word "limit" + just focus on the sky. on that great big blue + stretch my arms out into all of it.

"i did things others wanted me to do when i was younger + left out my wants..."

roll down a hill

i want to be fully present to my life + free to express my distinct presence. i want to let go of comparing myself to others + of trying to please them. i want to trust that being myself will be enough.

"...this gets me thinking that i might not want a serious relationship quite yet... i want to do some other things first like roll down a hill."

i will begin by choosing a delightful path to travel there. ride a go kart. walk barefoot across a beach. roll down a hill.

"i am a one woman act play + am now ready to challenge the other negative voices not belonging in my script."

my script

this life is my own + i am ready
to write it. to step into it + be.
fully. me.

my beloved messiness +
glorious flowers + weight of
love will be with me. i will trust
the great aquarium within +
follow my intuition. i will pay
attention to my emotions.
walk tall. drench myself in
goodness. fill my body with good
things. with the power of words +
action, i will create what i need +
cross over into love.

while this is a lot of work,
momentum is on my side, + my
path, delightful.

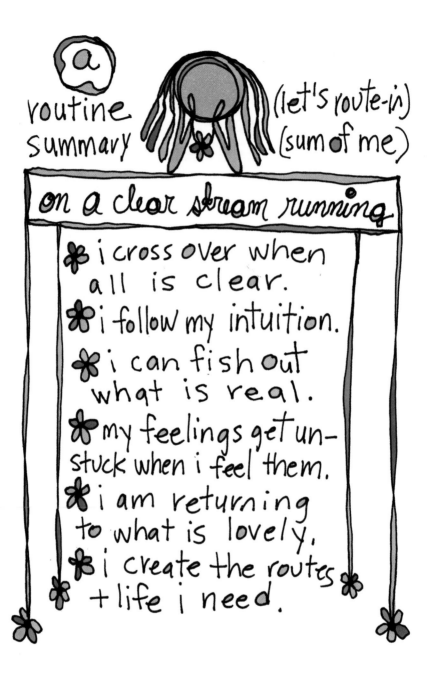

@
routine
summary   (let's route-in)
          (sum of me)

on a clear stream running.

* i cross over when all is clear.
* i follow my intuition.
* i can fish out what is real.
* my feelings get un-stuck when i feel them.
* i am returning to what is lovely.
* i create the routes + life i need.

* i am making best choices.
* my stomach feels good when i fill it with what is good.
* there is great power in getting going with something.
* pipes are good + so are my dreams.
* this is all my script.
* i am walking tall + rolling down hills.

"i've tried so hard
to not be
who i am

now i'm finally
living my life
for the first time
i am
who i am
who i am."

i am who i am who i am

i spent an afternoon with a group of
women. we had gathered to paint +
draw + share our life stories. toward
the end of the day, one of them
broke out in song. in full voice. she was
still in her chair. this was unplanned.
unannounced. yet she was just going
with it. going with being herself +
she looked completely comfortable +
her face, radiant.

i was completely captured + knew this
was why i was here. to see this. to
receive the invitation to be myself. to
know it is possible + beautiful.

there would be no turning back from
this knowledge. the music is now in my
bones + it is in yours too, dear one.

i am releasing
what does not belong
to me into the big sea.

let go

i kiss goodbye the material of
heaviness. the weight of shame.
excess doubt + all the dim on the in.
my awareness allows such release + i
am not so afraid anymore.

i am the bird now. of feather + wing
+ song. able to fly + sail + soar. across
oceans + prairies + finally home to
the peaceable kingdom of me.

"as i have
let go
of believing
i am
unloveable,
i have
also
let go
of
seventy five
pounds."

living out of beauty

i want to take the same care
with myself that beatrix
potter did in drawing peter
rabbit. i want to use soft
lines. loving words. kind
eyes. give myself sweet
pals. merry adventures.
fresh carrots.

i will begin by placing
colored pencils in my purse
to remind me.

"i have realized that i haven't been taking care of myself because i have been living out of my blah instead of my beauty."

to live out of

i am resolved

my beauty.

" it is
more
important
to be
myself
than
to be
right. "

be myself

i am learning from the
wild kingdom. from the
starfish in the depths
to the mountain goat
in the heights + all life
in between. who abide
in their strength. who
breathe into all they are
+ who are art on earth.

maybe our only business
is to be beautiful.

if you are looking, you will find me in the field of myself.

my words come out good

i am practicing saying words that come out of my heart. like they do before falling asleep. like they do when sitting with a trusted friend. like they do when writing next to a big lake.

i am paying attention to what happens when i give myself space to do this important work. the shower invites me to sing bigger. canyons coax me to be heard. it is how our world is made. it is how we are made.

"i liked what i said to a new group of people i was just with

because

i was less concerned with making an impression + more focused on speaking from my heart + when i do this, my words come out good."

i am changed
when i speak from my heart.✻

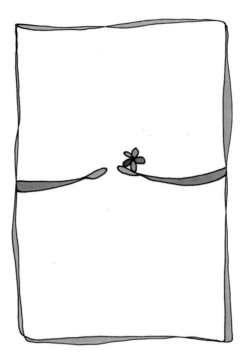

boundaries

i offer you a flower. it is full of my favorite colors.
golden yellow. chartreuse green. cadmium orange.
sea blue. true red. i offer it to you in an empty
room. where there is the peace of just you + me. so
you can really see it.

so you can really see me. so you can really see you.

"boundaries are
really about
sharing space
between people
for
giving + receiving
+ even i
with myself
need that space
to know
who
i am."

"i don't have
to look
at movie stars
+
compare myself
anymore
because
my life
is the epic...
just being me."

just being me

i awake. open my eyes. blood
courses through my veins.
oxygen fills my lungs. my head
thinks thoughts + heart chases
wisdom. my arms wrap around
life + lips say "you matter" + "i
love you". when pain comes, i
heal + when joy comes, i clap my
hands. when the sun goes down i
say "thank you" + melt back into
another evening of dreams.

this is epic enough for me.

what i invite

i want to go to the party of saint
francis + sow love where there
is hatred + hope where there is
despair. i want to dig deep into
my dna + unearth my
capacity. my strength.
my creative fire.

i want to burn brightly no
matter where i am.

"despite some of
the difficult people
in my life,
i am still
welcoming
authenticity,
serenity + joy...
it really comes
down to
not just who
is at my party
but what
i invite."

"i just heard myself say i have a bright inner light + i have never said that out loud before."

say out loud

i have read that speech + intelligence are related. that one strengthens + further develops the other.

so i want to say all my important words out loud + speak my way into deep knowing.

i am
speaking
of
my
bright
inner
light.

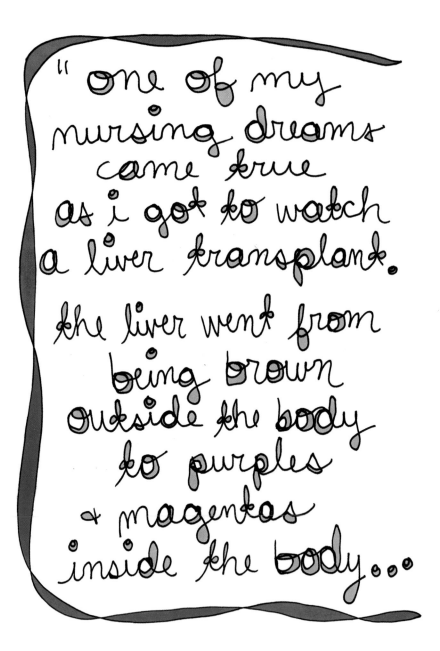

" one of my
nursing dreams
came true
as i got to watch
a liver transplant.

the liver went from
being brown
outside the body
to purples
+ magentas
inside the body...

what is inside us

cut open a watermelon. grapefruit. pineapple. find immediate delight in their juicy

insides. crack open a geode or an agate + find worlds of crystal wonderlands + swirling

colors + of course, there is the oyster's pearl.

...the surgeon
handled + stitched
with such reverence.
i now see
the rainbow
pales
in comparison
to what is
inside
us."

then there is the you + the me. our eyes + hair + ten fingers + toes are all a marvel.

then look inside + find all the rest of our greatest good. our stories held in our head +

heart + all our mounds of messy + all our luscious light.

"i want to meditate more on what saint teresa said that with God's eyes on us, we are reminded there is nothing wrong with us + never has been."

meditate more

what do your senses know of love? what has it smelled like? tasted. felt. sounded like? your grandpa's cigar or onions frying? chocolate + cheese? the smooth hair of a new doll + the rough trunk of a tree?

what does your heart know of love? i know mine understands that the smooth hair of a new doll would not find anything wrong with me. nor would the rough trunk of a tree. or anything else born of love.

i am looking through a lense of love.

dense + succulent

now that i see my insides
are juicy + beautiful, i am
beginning to
walk a watermelon life.
i am wearing more
colorful clothes. loving
extravagantly + doing
what i love to do.

this is the power of
listening + allowing +
really living my life.

"every piece of my day is dense + succulent."

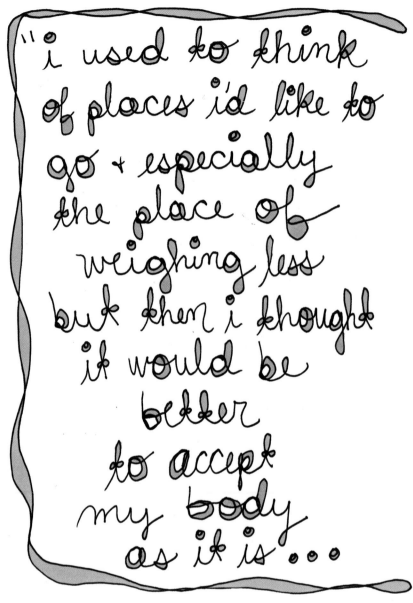

"i used to think
of places i'd like to
go + especially
the place of
weighing less
but then i thought
it would be
better
to accept
my body
as it is...

inside, here, now.

we have this invitation to be ourselves. to be about the business of being beautiful +
we have all that we need for the journey. we have our feathers + wings + song. our
capacity + strength + creative fire + our juicy insides.

... besides,
that place would
be outside of me
+ i prefer to
be inside,
here,
now."

we get to speak our most important things out of this place. we get to say the words that come out of our heart + love will tell us there is nothing wrong with us.

i offer you this flower.

@

routine summary (let's route-in) (sum of me)

on i am who i am who i am

* i am who i am.
* i am letting go of what does not belong to me.
* living out of my beauty is way better than out of my blah.
* it is more important to be myself than to be right.
* it always sounds good to speak from my heart.

* space between + within us helps us to know who we are.
* my life is the epic.
* (what) i invite to my party matters.
* i have a bright inner light.
* even rainbows pale in comparison to what is inside us.
* instead of what is wrong, i am focusing on my dense + succulent life.
* inside, here, now.

reflection questions

for self or small group discussion

messiness inside

what is a glimpse of my messiness? how do i see it in my
purse or closet or "junk" drawer? what stories of me are told
in these places? when i listen to my body, what sensations do i
feel + what stories are told there? how do i let laughter in? do
i need to let go of any belittling name-calling i tell myself? do
i see my beauty in my real story? what can i give myself in my
imagination? (lay on a hammock by the ocean to rest? walk
along a magical path in the woods?). what can i give myself in
my daily life? (reach out more? walks? a new journal?). what
are the messages in my life that i hear more than once? how
can i invite myself to feel all that is real inside? what are my
wide open doors?

creation out of chaos

do i sense something new for me in the rumblings of my life?
can i close my eyes to see? can i release what other people
wish for me + pay attention to my own listening within? do
i trust what i feel? what does it feel like inside when i hear
something that is false + something that is true? can i imagine
holding great compassion for all my heart goes through?
can i imagine loving myself as much as i could? can i imagine
stating such love + need into the beating of a drum? what gets
me up in the morning? how do i cultivate hope in my life?
what can i give to myself? (look up at the stars? take more
naps? write a poem in the middle of the afternoon?). how can
i affirm that good will come in the changes of my life? how do
i build strength? am i ready to release regret + embrace each
day as new? am i ready to get out of what does not serve me
anymore + get into the wholeness of me?

wake up

how awake am i to the wonder of my own life? do i taste the drippy bite of a peach? do i remember that a heart beats in my chest? am i present to the language of my dreams from the night? am i present to what i would love in my day if i dared to speak of it? how do i follow my heart? am i present to what is forming inside me + around me as i wait for certain things to unfold in my life? is it possible to find the gift in everything?

room for flowers

where do i see a need in my life for pruning? what would i be doing if i was making room for lovely things, such as mandalas + flowers? do i allow for spontaneous moments where beauty presents itself? how am i an active participant in creating more happiness? how do i intertwine with the good? am i willing to press on, even when not every effort is fruitful? how do i need extra loving care right now? am i embracing the various ingredients of my life that build me up? am i seeing i am continually renewed? do i see that my authentic life is my beautiful life? am i listening deeply? do my clothes match me? do i give myself permission to love what i love? to listen to my wants? to have my own opinions? am i awake to the wonderment of my life? how do i care for myself when I have days of flatness + no flow? how do i treasure my voice, my heart, my life?

hold hands

who are the people in my life who remind myself of myself? how do i offer thanks for connection with others + with myself? how do i sit with these feelings? who am i drawn to, when i imagine the bigness of our world? which famous people? animals? half-asleep encounters? company of the mysterious? how do i care for myself when i find connections more difficult? how do i release myself from the drive to fit in + free myself to stand out? do i let in people who are good to me? who connect + cluck in love? do i feel love's weight?

a clear stream running
how am i stepping into my life + following my intuition +
being myself? am i paying attention to my emotions? am i
walking tall? am i drenching myself in goodness? am i filling
my body with good things? what do i need to create? where
does my river need to travel? am i choosing what i believe
is my best? am i following my dreams? am i rolling down
the hills i want to + reading from the script of me? might i
consider free falling into such momentum?

i am who i am who i am
do i hear an invitation to be myself? to be in my strength
+ breathe into all i am? in what ways am i living out of my
beauty + in what ways out of my blah? can my awareness
allow me to let go of the weight of shame + doubt? am i
practicing speaking words that come out of my heart? no
matter where i am? am i amazed by my juicy insides? do
i look at myself through the lens of love? am i present to
myself right here + now? to my own epic tale? do i give
myself the space to see myself like the flower?